TALKABOUT VIDEO LIBRARY

MORE BRILLIANT PROFESSIONAL RESOURCES FROM BESTSELLING AUTHOR ALEX KELLY!

TALKABOUT

Each practical workbook in this bestselling series provides a clear programme of activities designed to improve self-awareness, self-esteem and social skills.

"All in all, Alex, what a wonderful world for kids it would be if your social skills programme were in all schools across the continents"- Catherine Varapodio Longley, Parent, Melbourne, 2013.

"I feel very lucky to work in a school where our pupils get the opportunity to utilise Talkabout resources and to see the benefit that this has made to them and their peers. You are making a difference!" – Nicole Thomas, Teacher, 2017

Title	Focus	Age-range
Talkabout (2nd edition)	Developing Social Skills for all ages	7+
Talkabout for Children 1 (2nd edition)	Developing Self-Awareness and Self-Esteem	4-11
Talkabout for Children 2 (2nd edition)	Developing Social Skills	4-11
Talkabout for Children 3 (2nd edition)	Developing Friendship Skills	4-11
Talkabout for Teenagers (2nd edition)	Developing Social and Emotional Communication Skills	11-19
Talkabout Transitions	Moving from education to employment	16+
Talkabout for Adults	Developing Self-awareness and Self-esteem in adults	16+
Talkabout Theory of Mind	Developing Social Skills and Relationships	11+
Talkabout Relationships	Developing Relationship Skills	11+
Talkabout Sex and Relationships 1	Developing Intimate Relationship Skills	11+
Talkabout Sex and Relationships 2	Sex Education	11+
Talkabout Assessment	Social Skills Assessment Tool	7+
Talkabout Video Library	Developing Social Skills	7+
Talkabout Board Game	Developing Social Communication skills, Self Esteem and Friendship Skills	7+
Talkabout Cards: Group Cohesion Games	Group Cohesion	7+
Talkabout Cards: Self Awareness Activities	Developing Self Awareness	7+

TALKABOUT VIDEO LIBRARY

SOCIAL COMMUNICATION SKILLS

ALEX KELLY

LONDON AND NEW YORK

First published 2006 by Speechmark Publishing Ltd. as *Talkabout DVD*

Published 2022 by Routledge as *Talkabout Video Library*
2 Park Square, Milton Park, Abingdon, Oxon OX14 4RN
605 Third Avenue Avenue, New York, NY 10017

Routledge is an imprint of the Taylor & Francis Group, an informa business

Copyright © Alex Kelly, 2006

All rights reserved. No part of this book may be reprinted or reproduced or utilised in any form or by any electronic, mechanical, or other means, now known or hereafter invented, including photocopying and recording, or in any information storage or retrieval system, without permission in writing from the publishers.

Product or corporate names may be trademarks or registered trademarks, and are used only for identification and explanation without intent to infringe.

Unauthorised recording, copying, loan, hire, public showing or broadcasting of the accompanying supplementary material is prohibited.

ISBN 978-1-032-29890-0 (pbk)

CONTENTS

Acknowledgements _____ vii
Introduction _____ viii

👤 PART 1 Talkabout Me and You

 1 Physical Appearance _____ 1
 2 Personality _____ 2

👤 PART 2 Talkabout Communication

 3 How do we communicate? _____ 3
 4 Body language _____ 4
 5 The way we talk _____ 4
 6 Conversational skills _____ 5
 7 Assertiveness skills _____ 6

👤 PART 3 Talkabout Body Language

 8 Body language _____ 8
 9 Eye contact _____ 10
10 Facial expression _____ 10
11 Hand gesture _____ 11
12 Distance _____ 12
13 Touch _____ 13
14 Fidgeting _____ 13
15 Posture _____ 14
16 Personal appearance _____ 15

👤 PART 4 Talkabout the Way We Talk

17 The way we talk _____ 16
18 Volume _____ 17
19 Rate _____ 18
20 Clarity _____ 18
21 Intonation _____ 19
22 Fluency _____ 19

CONTENTS

👤 PART 5 Talkabout Conversations

- **23** Conversational skills — **20**
- **24** Listening — **22**
- **25** Starting a conversation — **23**
- **26** Taking turns — **24**
- **27** Asking questions — **25**
- **28** Answering questions — **26**
- **29** Being relevant — **27**
- **30** Repairing — **28**
- **31** Ending a conversation — **29**

👤 PART 6 Talkabout Assertiveness

- **32** Assertiveness skills — **30**
- **33** Expressing feelings — **32**
- **34** Standing up for yourself — **33**
- **35** Making suggestions — **34**
- **36** Refusing — **35**
- **37** Disagreeing — **36**
- **38** Complaining — **37**
- **39** Apologising — **38**
- **40** Requesting explanations — **39**

ACKNOWLEDGEMENTS

I would like to thank the following people for their acting skills: Kavitha Babu, Ben Bissington, Emily Bridewell, Gareth Brown, Emma Browning, Naomi Carter, Adam Case, Sarah-Jayne Chase, Andrew Coombes, George Coombes, Mandy Coombes, Jack Copsy-Blake, Nadine Crew, Becca Davies, Joanne Drew, Bill Eales, Helen Eales, Jane Esmond, Michelle Fitchett, Matt Hampton, Lalla Hitchings, Tom Hitchings, Liane Hubbins, Ed Kelly, Peter Kelly, Nicholas King, Shelter Mhlanga, Andrew Moulster, Gwen Moulster, Steve Moulster, Sonia Osborne, Colin Pritchard, Donna Ravening, Cat Ray, Brian Sains, George Sains, Oliver Sheppard, Abigail Smith, Leah Warner-Ely and Rebecca Welsh.

Thank you also to Jonathan Leech for his support in this project and for his expertise with the sound and editing.

I would also like to thank Sytec Systems and Technology Ltd and The Trafalgar School at Downton for allowing me to film on their property.

As always, I would especially like to thank my husband, Brian Sains, for all his continuing support, encouragement and love.

INTRODUCTION

This product is intended to be used by teachers or therapists who are running social skills groups. It is not intended as a replacement to the social skills group but as an additional resource to be used within the group setting to help bring the different social skills to life. It is an essential resource for situations where there is only one group facilitator and therefore where it is difficult to model poor and good behaviour. This product is particularly useful for teachers/therapists using the Talkabout series, although can be used to complement any social skills programme.

The product contains acted scenarios for each skill being taught, modelling both poor and good behaviour. A variety of ages and settings has been used to stimulate different discussions. In this booklet there is a description of each scenario with teacher/therapist prompts for group discussion.

Visit *www.routledgetextbooks.com/textbooks/9781032298900/* to access the video library materials.

PART 1: TALKABOUT ME AND YOU

This section aims to improve awareness of self and others and includes scenarios on physical appearance and personality.

1 Physical Appearance

Description of scenario	Teacher prompts / discussion
Four female adults are standing in a row (Sonia, Gwen, Liane and Alex). Four male adults are standing in a row (Steve, Gareth, Andrew and Matt).	How could we describe these people? For example: sex, height, build, age, ethnicity.
Eight people are shown in individual clips: (a) Adult male – Brian (b) Elderly female – Helen (c) Young male child – George (d) Young female – Naomi (e) Middle aged male – Andrew (f) Elderly male – Bill (g) Middle aged female – Sonia (h) Male child – Peter	How could we describe these people? Consider: sex, age, build, hair, ethnicity, glasses, distinguishing features

• Talkabout Me and You •

2 Personality

Description of scenario	Teacher prompts / discussion
Two parents, a grandparent and two children are having a family meal. The camera pauses after different personalities are revealed: (a) Becca is happy, self confident, chatty. (b) Peter is naughty, attention seeking, bored. (c) Sarah-Jayne is stressed, bad-tempered, unfriendly. (d) Helen is kind, thoughtful, sensitive. (e) Brian is disinterested, antisocial, self-centred.	What words would you use to describe this person? What do you think he or she is like?
Six adults having a meal together. Throughout the meal the following personalities are revealed: (a) Gwen is outgoing, extravert and self-confident. (b) Becs is critical, bad-tempered and self-centred and Adam is kind, diplomatic and weak. (c) Colin is kind, thoughtful and sensitive and Shelter is shy and lacking self-confidence. (d) Andy is bored, antisocial and ill at ease.	What words would you use to describe these people? What do you think he or she is like?

PART 2: TALKABOUT COMMUNICATION

This section aims to explore what is involved in communication. It introduces group members to: how we communicate; body language; the way we talk (paralinguistic skills); conversational skills and assertiveness skills. Group members can then assess themselves on each skill using the rating charts in Talkabout.

3 How do we communicate?

Description of scenario	Teacher prompts / discussion
Four different people in separate clips show different ways of communicating: (a) Sarah-Jayne is *talking* to the camera. (b) Brian is *listening* on the telephone. (c) Ed is showing that he is tired and bored through his *body language*. (d) Helen is using *the way she talks* when shouting at Peter.	How is she or he communicating? What is she or he doing to communicate?
Sarah-Jayne, Donna, Lalla and Kavitha are chatting in a group. Clips from the scene show different ways of communicating: (a) Sarah-Jayne's use of body language. (b) Kavitha's listening. (c) The way Kavitha talks.	How do we communicate with each other? How are they communicating?

• Talkabout Communication •

4 Body language

Description of scenario	Teacher prompts / discussion
George, Ed, Peter, Becca and Emily are a group of teenagers talking and showing different aspects of body language. The stills show: (a) George's *facial expression*. (b) Peter's *eye contact*. (c) Becca's use of *gesture*. (d) Emily's *personal appearance*. (e) Ed's *posture*. (f) Emily's *fidgeting*. (g) Becca's use of *distance*. (h) Becca's use of *touch*.	How are they communicating? How are they using their bodies to communicate?

5 The way we talk

Description of scenario	Teacher prompts / discussion
Five different people in different clips showing different aspects of the way we talk to communicate: (a) *Rate:* Alex is talking at a fast rate. (b) *Volume:* Adam is talking using different levels of volume. (c) *Intonation:* Gareth is talking using a flat intonation. (d) *Fluency:* Shelter is talking in a dysfluent manner. (e) *Clarity:* Steve's speech is unclear.	How are they talking?

• Talkabout Communication •

6 Conversational skills

Description of scenario	Teacher prompts / discussion
Tom and Christine (Lalla) are having a conversation at a party.	
In the first scenario Tom and Christine both have inappropriate conversational skills.	How many things did you notice that were bad about that conversation?
Clips from the scene are then replayed to show the following inappropriate conversational skills: (a) Tom *starts the conversation inappropriately.* (b) Tom *asks too many questions* and some of these are inappropriate. (c) Tom goes off on a monologue and so does not *take turns.* (d) Tom does not *answer a question.* (e) Tom does not *listen* to something Christine says. (f) Tom says something that is not *relevant* to the conversation. (g) Christine does not correct (*repair*) Tom when he gets her name wrong. (h) Tom *ends the conversation inappropriately* by walking off.	
In the second scenario all aspects of conversational skills are appropriate (see above).	Is this a good conversation? What was good about it?

• *Talkabout Communication* •

7 Assertiveness skills

Description of scenario	Teacher prompts / discussion
Gwen, Adam and Colin are having an argument.	
The camera focuses on Gwen who is being aggressive. She is using a loud volume, an aggressive posture, she is not letting the other person explain and is putting them down.	What does being aggressive mean? How is Gwen behaving? How does Gwen appear? How do you think Colin and Adam feel?
The camera then focuses on Colin who is being passive. He is not speaking up for himself, he has poor posture, poor eye contact, his speech is quiet and dysfluent.	What does being passive mean? How is Colin behaving? How does Colin appear?
The camera then focuses on Adam who is being assertive. He talks calmly, clearly, has good posture and tries to resolve the argument.	What does being assertive mean? What is Adam doing that is different? How does Adam appear?

Talkabout Communication

7 Assertiveness skills continued

Description of scenario	Teacher prompts / discussion
There are eight different scenes that depict each assertiveness skill. (a) *Expressing feelings* – Helen is telling Sarah-Jayne how she is feeling. (b) *Apologising* – Gareth is apologising to Sonia for his behaviour yesterday. (c) *Complaining* – Adam is telephoning a bus company to complain. (d) *Disagreeing* – Tom and Lalla are disagreeing about the best route for a journey. (e) *Refusing* – Emily is unable to babysit for Mandy. (f) *Making suggestions* – Donna is making a suggestion to Kavitha about what to wear. (g) *Requesting explanations* – Ben is asking for an explanation in class. (h) *Standing up yourself* – Leah is standing up to Abigail and Michelle for being a vegetarian.	What is happening? What is the assertiveness skill?

PART 3:
TALKABOUT BODY LANGAGE

This section aims to explore all aspects of body language and to improve skills in relevant areas. This includes what is body language, eye contact, facial expression, hand gestures, distance, touch, fidgeting, posture and personal appearance.

8 Body language

Description of scenario	Teacher prompts / discussion
George, Ed, Peter, Becca and Emily are a group of teenagers talking and showing different aspects of body language. The stills show: (a) George's *facial expression*. (b) Peter's *eye contact*. (c) Becca's use of *gesture*. (d) Emily's *personal appearance*. (e) Ed's *posture*. (f) Emily's *fidgeting*. (g) Becca's use of *distance*. (h) Becca's use of *touch*.	How are they communicating? How are they using their body to communicate?

• Talkabout Body Language •

8 Body language continued

Description of scenario	Teacher prompts / discussion
Five scenarios that depict different feelings through body language and verbal skills: (a) *Anger* – Gareth and Adam are arguing following a small car accident in a car park (b) *Nervous* – Donna is waiting for the post to arrive (c) *Happy* – the post has arrived and Donna is happy (d) *Bored* – Sarah-Jayne and Helen are talking and Cat is bored (e) *Sad* – Lalla is watching a sad film	How are they feeling? How can we tell?
Five silent scenarios that depict different feelings non-verbally: (a) *Anger* – Ed and George are arguing. (b) *Nervous* – Ben is nervously waiting for something. (c) *Happy* – Abigail and Jack are excited. (d) *Bored* – Joanne is bored at school. (e) *Sad* – Michelle is sad.	How are they feeling? How can we tell?

• *Talkabout Body Language* •

9 Eye contact

Description of scenario	Teacher prompts / discussion
Helen and Adam are having a conversation at work. Helen starts the conversation.	
In the first scenario Adam uses very little eye contact and appears shy and evasive. The conversation dries up.	What is Adam's eye contact like? How does it make him appear? What should he do?
In the second scenario Adam uses too much eye contact which makes Helen feel uneasy and the conversation dries up.	What is Adam's eye contact like? How does it make him appear? What should he do?
In the third scenario Adam uses appropriate eye contact and the conversation goes well.	What is Adam's eye contact like? How does he appear? What is good about it?

10 Facial expression

Description of scenario	Teacher prompts / discussion
Andrew is talking about a new approach to rewarding non-sickness with an extra day's annual leave.	
Sonia uses no facial expression even though she thinks it's a really good idea.	What is Sonia's facial expression like? How does it make her appear? What should she do?
Gwen uses inappropriate facial expression that does not match with what she is saying.	What is Gwen's facial expression like? How does it make her appear? What should she do?
Liane has appropriate facial expression.	What is Liane's facial expression like? What is good about it?

Talkabout Body Language

11 Hand gesture

Description of scenario	Teacher prompts / discussion
Steve is giving a talk on drums.	
In the first scenario Steve uses no hand gestures. This is confusing and not helpful to the talk.	What is Steve's use of gesture like? How does he appear? What should he do?
In the second scenario Steve uses inappropriate hand gestures. These are distracting and confusing and not helpful to his talk.	What is Steve's use of gesture like? How does he appear? What should he do?
In the third scenario Steve uses appropriate hand gestures and the talk goes well.	What is Steve's use of gesture like? What is good about it?

Talkabout Body Language

12 Distance

Description of scenario	Teacher prompts / discussion
George and Ben are in a classroom at school. Joanne and Jack are also there.	
In the first scenario George comes and sits too close to Ben and asks him about his visit to the school nurse. Ben looks very uncomfortable and tries to move away.	What is George's use of distance like? How does it make him appear? How do you think Ben feels?
In the second scenario George sits far away from Ben. This is embarrassing for Ben and the others in the room.	What is George's use of distance like? How does it make him appear? How do you think Ben feels?
In the third scenario George sits at an appropriate distance from Ben and the conversation goes well.	What is George's use of distance like? What is good about it? What does good distance mean?

• Talkabout Body Language •

13 Touch

Description of scenario	Teacher prompts / discussion
Michelle and Abigail are in the playground. Abigail is upset.	
In the first scenario, Michelle uses too much touch and this makes Abigail feel uneasy.	What is Michelle's use of touch like? How does it make her appear? What should she have done? How do you think Abigail feels?
In the second scenario Michelle uses no touch.	What is Michelle's use of touch like? How does it make her appear? How do you think Abigail feels?
In the third scenario Michelle uses an appropriate amount of touch.	What is Michelle's use of touch like? What is good about it?

14 Fidgeting

Description of scenario	Teacher prompts / discussion
Gareth and Andrew are interviewing Steve.	
In the first scenario Steve fidgets a great deal. He appears nervous and his fidgeting is distracting.	What is Steve's fidgeting like? How does it make him appear? What should he do?
In the second scenario Steve does not fidget and appears more self-confident. The interview appears to go much better.	What is Steve's fidgeting like? What is good about it? How does he appear?

• Talkabout Body Language •

15 Posture

Description of scenario	Teacher prompts / discussion
Jane, the teacher, is talking about next term's school production. It is a relaxed school session and Ed, Abigail and Oliver are among the group of pupils.	
Ed's posture is inappropriately relaxed and laid back.	What is Ed's posture like? How does he appear?
Abigail's posture is too tense and rigid.	What is Abigail's posture like? How does she appear?
Oliver's posture is appropriate.	What is Oliver's posture like? What is good about it? How does he appear?

• Talkabout Body Language •

16 Personal appearance

Description of scenario	Teacher prompts / discussion
Andy and Shelter are going to the beach with Becs. It is a hot day and they are waiting for her. She comes downstairs in a thick cardigan and a woolly hat.	What is Bec's personal appearance like? How does she appear?
Steve arrives for an interview. He is wearing jeans and a T-shirt and is unshaven.	What is Steve's personal appearance like? How does he appear?
Becca and Emily are getting ready to go out for the evening. They are talking about what to wear.	What is important to think about with regard to our personal appearance? Consider: the weather, the situation, what you are hoping to achieve, what other people will think.

PART 4: TALKABOUT THE WAY WE TALK

This section aims to explore all aspects of the way we talk and to improve skills in relevant areas. This includes volume, rate, clarity, intonation and fluency.

17 The way we talk

Description of scenario	Teacher prompts / discussion
Five different people in different clips showing different aspects of the way we talk to communicate: (a) *Rate:* Alex is talking at a fast rate. (b) *Volume:* Adam is talking using different levels of volume. (c) *Intonation:* Gareth is talking using a flat intonation. (d) *Fluency:* Shelter is talking in a dysfluent manner. (e) *Clarity:* Steve's speech is unclear.	How are they talking?
Four people talk about how they're feeling: (a) Tom is angry about work. (b) Sarah-Jayne is bored. (c) Kavitha is nervous about an interview. (d) Donna is excited about going on holiday.	What is their speech like? Consider: rate, volume, intonation, fluency and clarity.

• Talkabout the Way We Talk •

17 **The way we talk** continued

Description of scenario	Teacher prompts / discussion
Four teenagers say the same thing and show their feelings through the way they say it. (a) George is angry. (b) Ed is bored. (c) Emily is nervous. (d) Becca is happy.	How are they feeling? How can you tell? What is their speech like?

18 Volume

Description of scenario	Teacher prompts / discussion
Andrew and Gareth are interviewing Steve.	
In the first scenario Andrew asks Steve a question in a loud volume. Steve is surprised.	What is Andrew's volume like? How does he appear? What should he do?
In the second scenario Andrew asks Steve a question in a low volume. Steve has to lean forward to hear it.	What is Andrew's volume like? How does he appear? What should he do?
In the third scenario Andrew asks Steve a question in an appropriate volume.	What is Andrew's volume like? What is good about it?

Talkabout the Way We Talk

19 Rate

Description of scenario	Teacher prompts / discussion
Jane, the teacher, is giving some homework to her class.	
In the first scenario Jane speaks at a very fast rate and the pupils find it difficult to make notes and keep up.	What is Jane's rate of speech like? How does she appear? What should she do?
In the second scenario Jane speaks too slowly and the pupils are bored.	What is Jane's rate of speech like? How does she appear? What should she do?
In the third scenario Jane speaks at an appropriate rate of speech.	What is Jane's rate of speech like? What is good about it?

20 Clarity

Description of scenario	Teacher prompts / discussion
Jane, the teacher, is asking about relationships and what is important in a relationship. She asks Jack what he thinks.	
In the first scenario Jack gives his answer but mumbles and is difficult to understand.	What is Jack's clarity of speech like? How does he appear? What should he do?
In the second scenario Jack speaks clearly and is easy to understand.	What is Jack's clarity of speech like? What is good about it?

• Talkabout the Way We Talk •

21 Intonation

Description of scenario	Teacher prompts / discussion
Jane, the teacher, asks if one of the pupils would like to give a talk about something they did over the summer holidays. Jane asks Nick to go first.	
In the first scenario Nick uses a very flat intonation, talking in a monotone. Everyone looks bored.	What is Nick's intonation like? How does he appear? What should he do?
In the second scenario Nick uses exaggerated intonation. Everyone looks confused and surprised.	What is Nick's intonation like? How does he appear? What should he do?
In the third scenario Nick uses appropriate intonation.	What is Nick's intonation like? What is good about it?

22 Fluency

Description of scenario	Teacher prompts / discussion
Gareth telephones Liane for some information which he needs quickly before going into a meeting.	
In the first scenario Liane has poor fluency. She pauses a great deal and is generally dysfluent. Gareth appears impatient and irritated.	What is Liane's fluency like? How does she appear? What should she do? How does Gareth feel?
In the second scenario Liane has good fluency. She gives the information fluently and Gareth is happy.	What is Liane's fluency like? What is good about it?

PART 5:
TALKABOUT CONVERSATIONS

This section aims to explore and improve conversational skills. This includes listening, starting a conversation, taking turns, asking questions, answering questions, being relevant, repairing a conversation and ending a conversation.

23 Conversational skills

Description of scenario	Teacher prompts / discussion
Tom and Christine (Lalla) are having a conversation at a party.	
In the first scenario Tom and Christine both have inappropriate conversational skills.	How many things did you notice that were bad about that conversation?
Clips from the scene are then replayed to show the following inappropriate conversational skills: (a) Tom *starts the conversation* inappropriately. (b) Tom *asks too many questions* and some of these are inappropriate. (c) Tom goes off on a monologue and so does not *take turns*. (d) Tom does not *answer a question*. (e) Tom does not *listen* to something Christine says.	

• Talkabout Conversations •

23 **Conversational skills** continued

Description of scenario	Teacher prompts / discussion
(f) Tom says something that is not *relevant* to the conversation. (g) Christine does not correct (*repair*) Tom when he gets her name wrong. (h) Tom *ends the conversation* inappropriately by walking off.	
In the second scenario all aspects of conversational skills are appropriate (see above).	Is this a good conversation? What is good about it?

• Talkabout Conversations •

24 Listening

Description of scenario	Teacher prompts / discussion
Gwen and Colin are at home. Gwen is cooking supper and Colin is working at his computer. Their son Andy arrives home from college. He is obviously worried about something that happened at college today and talks to his parents about it.	
In the first scenario Colin and Gwen both show poor listening skills.	Are Gwen and Colin listening? How does it make them appear? What should they do? How does Andy feel?
In the second scenario Gwen continues not to listen. This time Colin starts to listen but then interrupts and gives his opinion without hearing all the facts.	Are Gwen and Colin listening? How does it make them appear? What should they do?
In the third scenario both Colin and Gwen listen to Andy.	Are they listening? What is good about it? What shows someone that you're listening?

• Talkabout Conversations •

25 Starting a conversation

Description of scenario	Teacher prompts / discussion
It is Liane's first day at her new job. Andrew is showing Liane where she is going to sit and explains that Sonia shares the office and will mentor her for the first few weeks. Andrew then leaves and Sonia enters the room.	
In the first scenario Sonia starts a conversation with Liane inappropriately by going straight into a topic that is not appropriate.	What is Sonia like at starting the conversation? How does it make her appear? What should she do? How do you think Liane feels?
In the second scenario Sonia starts the conversation inappropriately by asking lots of questions.	What is Sonia like at starting the conversation? How does it make her appear? What should she do? How do you think Liane feels?
In the third scenario Sonia starts the conversation appropriately.	What is Sonia like at starting the conversation? What is good about it?

23

26 Taking turns

Description of scenario	Teacher prompts / discussion
Michelle, Abi and Leah are planning their weekend.	
In the first scenario Michelle does most of the planning and does not take turns. Leah tries to join in and say some things but Michelle does not let her. Abi appears happy to be quiet and let the others do the planning.	What is Michelle like at taking turns? How does it make her appear? What should she do? How do you think Leah feels?
In the second scenario Michelle and Leah take turns in the conversation and both are involved in planning the weekend. Abi is still quiet but is asked for her opinion.	What is Michelle like at taking turns? What is good about it?

Talkabout Conversations

27 Asking questions

Description of scenario	Teacher prompts / discussion
Adam and Shelter have been left alone together at a friend's house. Their friend is obviously trying to matchmake.	
In the first scenario Shelter tries to make conversation with Adam by asking him questions but he doesn't ask her any questions and so the conversation is very one sided.	What is Adam like at asking questions? How does it make him appear? What should he do? How do you think Shelter feels?
In the second scenario Adam asks Shelter lots of questions but some of these are inappropriate.	What is Adam like at asking questions? How does it make him appear? What should he do? How do you think Shelter feels?
In the third scenario both Adam and Shelter ask each other questions and the conversation is much easier.	What is Adam like at asking questions? What is good about it?

• Talkabout Conversations •

28 Answering questions

Description of scenario	Teacher prompts / discussion
Jane, the teacher, wants to have a one-to-one chat with Oliver to find out if he is settling into his new school.	
In the first scenario Jane tries to find out how Oliver is getting on but Oliver does not answer any of her questions fully. He uses a lot of gesture and short phrases.	What is Oliver like at answering questions? How does it make him appear? What should he do? How do you think Jane feels?
In the second scenario Oliver doesn't listen to the question and answers the first question inappropriately.	What is Oliver like at answering questions? How does it make him appear? What should he do? How do you think Jane feels?
In the third scenario Oliver answers Jane's questions appropriately.	What is Oliver like at answering questions? What is good about it?

• Talkabout Conversations •

29 Being relevant

Description of scenario	Teacher prompts / discussion
Gareth and Steve are in a meeting with four others. Gareth wants to talk about time off at Christmas.	
In the first scenario Steve starts to talk about tea and coffee money, which is irrelevant to the conversation. Gareth tries to bring the conversation back to time off at Christmas but Steve continues to be irrelevant.	What is Steve like at being relevant? How does it make him appear? What should he do?
In the second scenario Steve asks appropriately that tea and coffee money is discussed and Gareth agrees to add it to the agenda. Steve is therefore relevant and appropriate.	What is Steve like at being relevant? What is good about it?

• Talkabout Conversations •

30 Repairing

Description of scenario	Teacher prompts / discussion
Sonia and Liane are talking about Liane's first day at work and Sonia is finding out how Liane has enjoyed it. Andrew, their manager, then walks in.	
In the first scenario Andrew asks Liane if she has enjoyed her first day but calls her Laura instead of Liane. Liane does not correct him and so does not repair the conversation.	What is Liane like at repairing the conversation? How does it make her appear? What should she do? What could happen if Liane doesn't correct Andrew?
In the second scenario Liane corrects Andrew appropriately and therefore repairs the conversation.	What is Liane like at repairing the conversation? What is good about it?

• Talkabout Conversations •

31 Ending a conversation

Description of scenario	Teacher prompts / discussion
Tom and Kavitha are talking at a party.	
In the first scenario Tom suddenly walks off in the middle of the conversation.	What is Tom like at ending the conversation? How does it make him appear? What should he do? How do you think Kavitha feels?
In the second scenario Tom ends the conversation appropriately.	What is Tom like at ending the conversation? What is good about it?

PART 6: TALKABOUT ASSERTIVENESS

This section aims to explore and improve assertiveness skills. This includes expressing feelings, standing up for yourself, making suggestions, refusing, disagreeing, complaining, apologising and requesting explanations.

32 Assertiveness skills

Description of scenario	Teacher prompts / discussion
Andrew, Steve's line manager, is talking to Steve about cancelling his annual leave due to work pressures.	
In the first scenario Steve tries to protest, as he has a holiday booked with his family, but eventually agrees to cancel his holiday and come into work. He is behaving in a passive manner.	What is Steve's behaviour like? Is he being assertive? How does he appear? What should he do?
In the second scenario Steve responds to Andrew's request in an aggressive manner. He is quick to criticise Andrew's request and uses aggressive body language.	What is Steve's behaviour like? Is he being assertive? How does he appear? What should he do?
In the third scenario Steve responds to Andrew's request appropriately. He listens to Andrew and refuses in an assertive manner. He also looks for some compromise to help Andrew with the work.	What is Steve's behaviour like? Is he being assertive? How can you tell? How does he appear? What is good about it?

• Talkabout Assertiveness •

32 Assertiveness skills continued

Description of scenario	Teacher prompts / discussion
Cat has telephoned Becca to tell her that Becca has to come round on Saturday night because Cat's plans have fallen through and she'll be on her own.	
In the first scenario Becca tries to say that she can't come because she already has plans with Anna but eventually agrees to cancel her plans. She is behaving in a passive manner.	What is Becca's behaviour like? Is she being assertive? How does she appear? What should she do?
In the second scenario Becca responds to Cat in an aggressive manner. She does not consider Cat's request and does not intend to cancel or change her arrangements.	What is Becca's behaviour like? Is she being assertive? How does she appear? What should she do?
In the third scenario Becca responds to Cat's request appropriately and assertively. She listens to Cat and explains that she has already made plans but then invites Cat to join in with her plans.	What is Becca's behaviour like? Is she being assertive? How can you tell? How does she appear? What is good about it?

Talkabout Assertiveness

33 Expressing feelings

Description of scenario	Teacher prompts / discussion
Sarah-Jayne is in the kitchen when Tom arrives home four hours late from work. Sarah-Jayne has prepared supper for them and Tom informs her that he has already eaten. Sarah-Jayne is angry and upset.	
In the first scenario Sarah-Jayne does not express her feelings effectively. She ends up apologising and says she will eat on her own. She is behaving in a passive manner.	Is Sarah-Jayne able to express her feelings effectively? How does it make her appear? What should she do?
In the second scenario Sarah-Jayne does not express her feelings effectively. She is immediately aggressive and tells Tom how she is feeling using aggressive verbal and non-verbal behaviour.	Is Sarah-Jayne able to express her feelings effectively? How does it make her appear? What should she do?
In the third scenario Sarah-Jayne responds appropriately and is able to express her feelings in an assertive manner. She explains how she feels and suggests what Tom could do in future.	Is Sarah-Jayne able to express her feelings effectively? How can you tell? How does it make her appear? What is good about it?

• Talkabout Assertiveness •

34 Standing up for yourself

Description of scenario	Teacher prompts / discussion
Adam, Gareth and Steve are talking in the kitchen at work. Gareth and Steve start discussing another work colleague who they have discovered goes to church. They then find out that Adam also goes to church and are critical that he is not able to play football with them on Sunday.	
In the first scenario Adam does not stand up for himself when they tease him about going to church. He appears weak. He is behaving in a passive manner.	Is Adam standing up for himself? How does he appear? What should he do?
In the second scenario Adam responds in an aggressive manner. He is quick to criticise the others' lack of faith and uses aggressive body language.	Is Adam standing up for himself? How does he appear? What should he do?
In the third scenario Adam stands up for himself appropriately. He explains his opinion in an assertive manner.	Is Adam standing up for himself? How can you tell? How does he appear? What is good about it?

• Talkabout Assertiveness •

35 Making suggestions

Description of scenario	Teacher prompts / discussion
George, Ed, Becca and Emily are planning what they should do tonight. Most of the group would like to go clubbing but George doesn't want to. He'd prefer to do something cheaper.	
In the first scenario George does not manage to make his suggestion effectively and they decide to go clubbing. He appears weak and is behaving in a passive manner.	Is George able to make suggestions? How does he appear? What should he do?
In the second scenario George responds to the group's suggestions in an aggressive manner. He is quick to criticise the others and uses aggressive verbal and non-verbal behaviour.	Is George able to make suggestions? How does he appear? What should he do?
In the third scenario George makes his suggestions appropriately and in an assertive manner. He explains why he'd prefer not to go clubbing and suggests a compromise.	Is George able to make suggestions? How can you tell? How does he appear? What is good about it?

• Talkabout Assertiveness •

36 Refusing

Description of scenario	Teacher prompts / discussion
Oliver and Leah are outside in the school playground. Oliver offers Leah a cigarette which she does not want.	
In the first scenario Leah finds it difficult to refuse effectively. She appears weak and lacking in confidence.	Is Leah able to refuse effectively? How does she appear? What should she do?
In the second scenario Leah refuses in an aggressive manner. She is rude to Oliver and criticises the fact that he smokes. She appears aggressive.	Is Leah able to refuse effectively? How does she appear? What should she do?
In the third scenario Leah refuses appropriately and in an assertive manner.	Is Leah able to refuse effectively? How can you tell? How does she appear? What is good about it?

• Talkabout Assertiveness •

37 Disagreeing

Description of scenario	Teacher prompts / discussion
Colin and Becs are buying a house together and Becs has seen some furniture that she'd like to buy from a catalogue. Colin is unhappy about it and disagrees with Becs because they do not have a lot of money and they had agreed not to get into debt.	
In the first scenario Colin does not disagree effectively with Becs and she ends up ordering the furniture. He appears weak and is behaving in a passive manner.	Is Colin disagreeing effectively? How does he appear? What should he do?
In the second scenario Colin disagrees with Becs in an aggressive manner. He doesn't listen to her and immediately criticises her choices. He uses aggressive verbal and non-verbal behaviour.	Is Colin disagreeing effectively? How does he appear? What should he do?
In the third scenario Colin disagrees with Becs appropriately. He listens to her and then explains his opinion in an assertive manner.	Is Colin disagreeing effectively? How can you tell? How does he appear? What is good about it?

• Talkabout Assertiveness •

38 Complaining

Description of scenario	Teacher prompts / discussion
Colin is going over to his neighbour Adam's house to complain about the noise last night.	
In the first scenario Colin does not complain effectively and apologises for waking Adam. He appears weak and behaves in a passive manner.	Is Colin complaining effectively? How does he appear? What should he do?
In the second scenario Colin complains in an aggressive manner. He uses aggressive verbal and non-verbal behaviour.	Is Colin complaining effectively? How does he appear? What should he do?
In the third scenario Colin complains appropriately. He explains how he's feeling in an assertive manner.	Is Colin complaining effectively? How can you tell? How does he appear? What is good about it?

• Talkabout Assertiveness •

39 Apologising

Description of scenario	Teacher prompts / discussion
Sarah-Jayne is on the telephone to her friend. She is apologising for her behaviour last night when she was rude about her friend's weight.	
In the first scenario Sarah-Jayne receives the phone call and apologises for her behaviour inappropriately. She continues to criticise her friend's choice of clothes and offers advice about dieting.	Is Sarah-Jayne apologising effectively? How does she appear? How do you think her friend feels? What should she do?
In the second scenario Sarah-Jayne telephones her friend and immediately apologises appropriately and assertively for her behaviour.	Is Sarah-Jayne apologising effectively? How can you tell? How does she appear? What is good about it? What did she do differently?

• Talkabout Assertiveness •

40 Requesting explanations

Description of scenario	Teacher prompts / discussion
Jane, the teacher, is explaining something to the class. Emma obviously does not understand what Jane is explaining.	
In the first scenario Jane asks if all the children understand and they all say yes except for Emma who says no. When Jane asks Emma if she needs her to explain again, Emma says no and does not request an explanation. She behaves in an embarrassed and passive manner.	Is Emma requesting an explanation effectively? How does she appear? What should she do?
In the second scenario Emma requests an explanation in an aggressive manner. She mutters under her breath to her friend and then uses aggressive verbal and non verbal behaviour.	Is Emma requesting an explanation effectively? How does she appear? What should she do?
In the third scenario Emma requests an explanation appropriately and in an assertive manner.	Is Emma requesting an explanation effectively? How can you tell? How does she appear? What is good about it?